Jack
Baker Street

Written by Jill Eggleton
Illustrated by Philip Webb

Baker Street was a neat street.
The people in Baker Street
cut their grass,
washed their cars
and weeded their gardens
every week.

2

Baker Street
was a neat street
until . . .

Jacko came.

3

Jacko had an old, red truck.
It was so old
he couldn't drive it.
He put it in front of his house
and the grass grew under it.

4

Sometimes,
Jacko washed his truck.
He made soap bubbles
as big as balloons and
they floated down Baker Street.
The kids in Baker Street
could never catch them.

Jacko cut his grass,
but not like the other people
in Baker Street.
He cut circles and squares
and triangles in it.

The other people
in Baker Street had flowers
in their gardens,
but Jacko had weeds.
"I like weeds," said Jacko.
And he let them grow
as big as trees!

7

The kids in Baker Street
liked Jacko.
He made things for them.
He got this and that
from his old truck
and he made moon buggies.

8

The kids loved
those moon buggies.
They whizzed
up and down Baker Street.
"Moon buggies are cool,"
they said.

9

Jacko liked making things
for the kids in Baker Street.
He got ropes and old tyres,
and made swings in the trees.
He got this and that
from his old shed . . .

10

and he made kites
with funny faces.
The kids *flew* those kites
up and down Baker Street.

11

But Mr Little in Baker Street said, "This street was neat until Jacko came."
So he got some paper and he put . . .

Baker Street Petition

We want a neat street.
We don't want Jacko in our street.
Please put your name and address here.

Name	Address
T. Little	4 Baker Street

The people of Baker Street
looked at the petition.
"No," they said. "We like Jacko
and we like him in our street.
We will not put our names
on that petition."

Jacko was so pleased
he gave all the people
in Baker Street
a big bunch of weeds
from his garden!
Mr Little got a bunch of
weeds, too!

A Petition

Baker Street Petition

Please put your name on this petition if you like Jacko in our street.

Name	Address
Jillian Smith	1 Baker Street
Joanna Green	7 Baker Street
Tim Black	8 Baker Street
Sam Beal	4 Baker Street
Joe Nightingale	10 Baker Street
Trevor Nelson	6 Baker Street
Kyle Underwood	5 Baker Street

▬▬ Guide Notes

Title: Jacko of Baker Street
Stage: Early (4) – Green

Genre: Fiction
Approach: Guided Reading
Processes: Thinking Critically, Exploring Language, Processing Information
Written and Visual Focus: Petition
Word Count: 340

THINKING CRITICALLY
(sample questions)
- What do you think this story could be about?
- Look at pages 2 and 3. What do you notice about the people in Baker Street?
- Look at pages 4 and 5. What do you notice about Jacko?
- Look at pages 8 and 9. What could Jacko's neighbour be thinking about him?
- Look at pages 12 and 13. What do you think Mr Little could be saying to the people?

EXPLORING LANGUAGE

Terminology
Title, cover, illustrations, author, illustrator, title page

Vocabulary
Interest words: weeded, buggies, petition, address
High-frequency words (new): until, catch, never

Print Conventions
Capital letter for sentence beginnings, title, names (**J**acko, **M**r **L**ittle) and place names (**B**aker **S**treet), full stops, exclamation marks, quotation marks, commas, ellipses